Beneath the Falls

Beneath the Falls

POEMS

Mark D. Bennion

RESOURCE *Publications* · Eugene, Oregon

BENEATH THE FALLS
Poems

Resource Publications
An Imprint of Wipf and Stock Publishers
199 W. 8th Ave., Suite 3
Eugene, OR 97401

www.wipfandstock.com

PAPERBACK ISBN: 978-1-7252-8226-1
HARDCOVER ISBN: 978-1-7252-8227-8
EBOOK ISBN: 978-1-7252-8228-5

Manufactured in the U.S.A.   12/03/20

For Kristine, Elena, Karen, Mirah, Brynn, and Brian

Grateful to stand with you all beneath the falls

Contents

Acknowledgments and Permissions

Versions of these poems have appeared in the following publications. I express gratitude to the editors of these journals for their interest, suggestions, and support.

Aethlon, "Fifth Set," "Ironman," and "Sweetness"

AIM-America's Intercultural Magazine, "Summer Wish from a Bedouin Tent"

Anglican Theological Review, "Good Friday"

BYU Studies Quarterly, "Back," "The Night Before My Baptism," "Rabbi, Where Dwellest Thou?" "Silent Wednesday," and "Spirit"

Camas, "Beneath the Falls"

Comstock Review, "Letulogy"

Contemporary American Voices, "Denial," "Grass," and "Imagining You the Morning After My Birth"

The Cresset, "Semblance" and "I am here, Lord"

Dappled Things, "Playing Ball at Church"

Dialogue: A Journal of Mormon Thought, "My Brother's Bed" and "Seeing Someone I Used to Know"

Furrow, "Tween"

Ink & Letters, "End of the Season"

On the Warm Sands of the Tongue, "The Dark Room"

The Penwood Review, "Holding It Together"

Perspective, "Considering What's Undone" and "The Language of Conversion"

RHINO, "Alive Serious," "On the Anniversary of Your Death" (originally titled "Dear Brian"), and "On the Edge of It"

River Oak Review, "First Day of School"

Shemom, "Pregnancy" and "The Reader"

Spiritus, "Arrival—Fall 2001"

Tailwind, "Speechless"

Third Wednesday, "Braiding My Daughter's Hair"

Time of Singing, "Supplication"

Windhover: a Journal of Christian Literature, "Holding Your Hand in Bed," "Recap," "Sacrament," "Straightway," and "Totality"

"My Brother's Bed" also appeared in *Psalm & Selah: a poetic journey through the Book of Mormon* (2009, Bentley Enterprises). This poem and "On the Anniversary of Your Death" were published in *Forsythia* (2013, Aldrich Press).

"Sweetness" is for the Chicago Bears' running back Walter Payton (1954–1999), and "Totality" owes a debt to Annie Dillard's essay "Total Eclipse."

In mulling over this collection, I think first and foremost of Patricia Goedicke (1931–2006) who mentored me along the first steps of my graduate school education. Her vision, incisiveness, and nudging set a number of these poems in motion, giving them just the right push. Greg Pape's workshops at the University of Montana were and continue to be a boon to my poetic process. His guidance and encouragement have been immeasurable. Paul Zimmer is another wonderful mentor and friend whose frank appraisal has improved specific work in this collection. The Brigham Young University-Idaho administration, English Department colleagues, and my students have been supportive of my efforts as both a teacher and writer. Their goodwill, monetary support, suggestions, and interest in this project strengthened me, especially when my belief in it halted.

During the Spring 2019 semester at BYU-Idaho, Dr. Quinn Grover and his editing class offered valuable feedback. They provided me with solid, objective distance from these poems and offered perceptive criticism regarding the organization of this book. I also extend appreciation to Tyler Blanchard, Ashley Chilcutt, Michelle

Grooms, Aubrey Manwaring, Tyler Oswald, and Mason Stoddard for sharing editorial advice and additional views of these poems.

I can't thank my family enough for dealing with a poet in their midst: my parents for instilling in me a love for the creative word and the Word; my siblings for their humor, interest, and kindness; my in-laws for their generosity and perspective. Always, gratitude to and love for my wife, Kristine—my strongest supporter, editor, and inspiration. Her buoyant optimism, sharp intuition, and constant sacrifices are unending wells of water in times of plenty and drought. Finally, much love to my children who continue to show me that poetry isn't just a right mix of words or a birthday gift, it's a way to live and breathe.

Author's Note

Most of these poems arise out of autobiographical experience, memory, conversation, gesture: the electric, the mundane, and everything in between. Invariably, I have grappled with how to effectively blend specific narratives and aesthetic choices. What do I leave in, and what do I take out? What do I sacrifice for the good of the poem? When do I privilege memory above an artistic decision? Hence, in pondering these questions and considering the demands of some poems, I have altered the truth of the experience—or on occasion combined experiences—for the larger truth of thematic insight. Please know my intent is not to change history or be deceptive. Rather, I have tried to be as honest as possible in developing the ideas and epiphanies within each poem. Thank you in advance for understanding and for taking a chance on this book. Happy reading!

Nativity

Imagining You the Morning After My Birth

You cradle me in the yellow haze
after a fitful night. Your stomach
still ablaze with uterine contractions
as I learn how to eat. The St. Mary
nurses coo and question, juggle IV's
and needles, medicine and bed sheets.
You look for yourself and your parents
in my swollen face, measure this fist against
your pointer finger. There are shivers

of hunger passing between us, muscles
that will take another three trimesters to heal.
With one hand you trace the cartilage
and sinew along the ridges of my nose
and chin, with the other you prop up
my neck and witness my effort to swallow.
From the other rooms come staid, doctored
voices and intermittent moans. You'd pray
for these women—your sisters now in their terror—

in their offering of blood, lungs, and bone,
but it's all you can do to remember
the next visitor as your head begins to nod,
bobbing to the even rhythms of sleep.
I hear your regular heartbeat and open one eye
toward the hunch of your shoulder
and wrinkled hospital gown. Your hair is matted
with the strains of yesterday's sweat, the strands
of blond tucked in by exhaustion as you take

this moment for yourself, this necessary
point of departure, like a ship heading
for the sea. In days to come, I'll receive
the newspaper praise and starboard attention
from my brothers. Yet in the core of wrinkles
and puppet fingers, in the jolts and stops
of this flesh and the scarred emblems
of your body, we know the real star
of the past nine months—a constellation

I am just now beginning to see.

The Night Before My Baptism

I pull the sheets away from the pillows,
turn down the bed lamp, the blinds,
as a thick clattering rain
pours from the mountains and leaves its spattering

on my roof. Thunder mushrooms in the valley,
lightning divides the dimness in my room,
a rocket flash. I think how each drop
might scatter the loose tiles above me, rinsing

the gutters. Mulch, berries, and dead mice
rattle eaves before they fall to the ground.
The bed shakes me, the chatter turns to rumble,
but I fasten in, grind down, and believe.

Tween

Too young for the swagger
of my older brothers and too old
for the loose teeth of my sister,

I would go to the solace
of baseball cards, the surety
of their stats: Mickey Mantle's

536 homers, Nolan Ryan's
fifth no-hitter against the Dodgers,
Carew's .388 batting average in 1977.

What was in that fixation,
that finessed search, that witness
of another player's numbers?

I remember hours flipping
over each card, mouthing
"Tenace the Menace"

or not knowing how to pronounce
"Vida" in Vida Blue. The same
care turned to managers:

Harvey Kuenn's tobacco, Sparky Anderson's
shift from the National to American League,
Rose's figure as player and gambler.

All I needed was an afternoon
to consider a few hits,
compare the Braves' home runs

with the Phillies', number
Henderson's stolen bases
after he eclipsed the grace

of Lou Brock, see fans
in the right field of Wrigley
or Comiskey poking through

the white walls of my room,
and linger there through dinner
until the bottom of the ninth

when the crowd's roar
channeled through me,
as if I wore my own uniform

under early evening lights,
my brothers look on from the stands,
my sister hands me a bat.

Football Practice

My brothers warned me about practicing
twice-a-day in August. All July
I slept from dawn till noon.
Their voices called down to my room:

Lift weights! Swim laps. Go clean the garage.
Their knowledge was a sandpaper kiss.
One morning before light scorched mist
from the horizon, they woke me,

flinging the door open, denting the wall,
Time to go. I groveled out of the sack
and caught a ride to the field
with their cleats around my neck.

I found a helmet that was almost snug,
then picked up pants still green
from the last season's stain. My buddies
and I dressed in the throb of dawn.

On the field, we ran sweeps
across the fifty-yard line and wiped sweat
on the palms of each other's hands.
I kept hearing my brothers

growl through my mouthguard.
I knew that they could throw the ball
the length of twenty cars. My breathing
revealed my workless summer.

Dry air sucked vapor from my body.
My missed blocks turned to sprints
as my friends hurdled trash cans,
charged a fountain like the Gadarene herd.

I chewed water out of a blade of grass.
The water boys laughed. Not even
a cold shower could stop my sweating.
Coach's voice burned like fat on a grill,

Show up tonight by six o'clock.
I limped home through muscle spasms
that raked from groin to ankle. Sweat burrowed
in my eye, stung the left side of my face.

I kept hoping my brothers wouldn't be home.
I kept hoping my arms wouldn't shake.
When I stumbled through the screen door,
I knocked over the ironing board

and sprawled across the laundry room carpet.
I couldn't hear the air conditioner's grind,
nor feel my brothers' hands as they pulled
me up off the floor.

Pearl

My sixty-year-old boss swings
        with a dying pendulum's grace
                as she lifts plastic bags
from street corners,
        waddles against
                the sun's descent.
Her body's gears
        propel her from parks
                to carports. She charts
the gravel roads
        by the cans she picks up.
                Fingers, nicked from dog bites,
cling to unhooked,
        steering-wheels greased
                with fiberglass and oil;
the big knuckles,
        cracked pink and raw,
                move to the slightest
edge of barrow pits.
        Sometimes she speaks
                of what her three ex-husbands
gathered: honey,
        dictionaries, trampolines
                from the Badlands

and Florida swamps.
        The push of hormones was their gift.
            They worshipped junk bonds
and bets—
        leaving a family to grind
            after they'd gone.
She hauls long
        light bulbs at dusk,
            slimy among the leaves,
her quick sweep of mulch
        into the dump's burning,
            a truck's last sputter,
the rust.
        Her exes return in lantern light,
            spinning for children, meat loaf,
until they ramble
        through excuse, and re-excuse.
            Their hard heads she knocks against.
She juggles their pain, then spits
        as it echoes out of her heart,
            out of her wild hive.

End of the Season

The hems of our jerseys, drenched with grass stains
and sweat, hung on our bodies, splayed, reeking.
We moved slow and contrite along the vein
of the bus and sulked home without feeling
our feet or breath. The coach moaned praises
through half-hearted spit. *Dave done threw the ball*
real well. I didn't see nothin' lazy
out there today. His voice grew stiff and bald,
ignoring the scoreboard truth. The sky flushed
along its rim, carrying our slurred shame
of missed tackles and fumbled balls. Our hushed
disappointment turned to snivels of pain.
We said, *Next year*, trying to load the dice.
We huddled with that thought all through the night.

On the Edge of It

1.

At nineteen, on the rise
of friendship with my parents,
I walked beside a body
of water. I saw it. It wasn't
the first time, but I saw it,
the waves coming close in the evening.
Mom stooped at the bathroom sink,
hair fell from the crown
of her head, clumping in the drain.
She slumped at the dinner table,
her soup a glassy lake, the corn
like kidney stones. I was nineteen.
I said, *You must eat.*

2.

I left home and flew
to the world's edge. I imagined
her when I met a man
with a mushroom growing
on his neck; a purple spot covered
his left temple. His eyes kept
watering. He ran a finger
over my name tag, stroked
my white shirt. His palms
were the color of lye. But I
was blind then and preached,
Rain will flood the highest streets
in July and December. All gutters
will splash flowers and weeds.
And I moved on.

3.

It is raining and I see her
at the kitchen table. I write
a letter to ask her forgiveness.
I write with an iron pen.
Mom leans over
eating tomatoes and lettuce.
A mush melon is sliced open.
She moves slowly to the window,
follows the torrents to the ground.
She knows her weight. She cleans
her hands, hides her strange breath.

4.

When Mom suggests we go swimming,
we head straight for the ocean.
She dives into the waves, but the kelp
and brine drag her to the coral's reef.
I shout for the lifeguard
and start to wade in.
I promise not to tell;
she promises to reach the shore.
The guard throws a life vest
close to my mother's hands.
Once she grabs it,
her body flips in the rushing tide.

Speechless

> Shadows of Scott's hands
> bounce across the kitchen wall
> as he teaches me Sign.

After dinner my roommate mutters, *You remember spell your name ASL?* It's the fifth time he's asked me in the past two days. I snarl at my fingers and spell "M" and "A" with a teacher's ease but can't recall how to make "R" and "K." I arch my fingers back into swirling configurations, and then my wrist goes limp. I shrug and begin to play with the remaining rice on my plate. *Do again*, he manages. His voice sounds full of watermelon.

> *Mark, why don't study?*
> *You learn fast, show others how.*
> *We make large classes.*

I nod under the swift buzz of kitchen light. Scott keeps his eyes fixed on my lips as I raise my head and look past him out the window. He follows my gaze into a brick wall. I feel like the older brother trying to divert his attention so I can snatch food off his plate. A spider makes its way out from under the table.

> Scott's been deaf ten years.
> He's studied sign for seven.
> I think: *ignition.*

I hold up my pointer finger to let him know I'll be back soon. The doorknob feels greasy in my hand. I walk by some friends laughing hysterically. The ripping and snorts catch in their noses. They stoop, gripping the sweet ache and eventually succumb to the ground as I recall catch phrases and introductions.

Mark, you play football?
I played three years in high school.
You want to throw ball, now?

I return after midnight. Scott glances at me, then resumes watching TV. The closed captioning reflects off the living room posters, blocks hard in his eyes. He mouths the rush of white words. He crosses his arms like a little child. I'm tempted to ask about the actual cause of his deafness.

Mark, I wait five hours.
What you been doing all night?
Everywhere I look.

From our room comes the shaking thud of bass rhythms. Zeppelin's boom and assertion rattle the change and golf tees on my shelf. A quick thrust of car lights shimmies through the window and scampers away. His hands press against a speaker. Vibrations hollow out the wall.

Most nights come to this:
loam flashes, notepads reeling.
His thumbs like rockets.

Arrival

When I left for Jerusalem
and the Holy Land bustle,
orthodox lions, a prophet's zeal
for the psalm soared in me—
a hymn of praise I carried
above the Mediterranean. I spoke
peace to the flight attendant
and prayed between sleep, head
dipping and nodding, eyes bulging
in text, quickly smiling
at my fellow passengers, breath secured,
bags stashed, tray table
tapping against my chest.

Before the plane touched down
I saw light dip in the ocean waves.
On the roads of Tel Aviv,
I flagged down a cab,
babbled out to the driver, threw
my luggage in back, nose-dived
into the car's front-seat.
My body burned as if riding
near the edge of a cliff,
and then out of the gears' staccato
the muffler roared,
and the half-rolled window
stuck in the humid air;
hung like a distant horizon
streaked with water marks, tobacco,
mountain tips; and shook
in the car's idle again and again.

At a red light I noticed a man
holding a sign: *I lost my home*
in a recent attack.
His body swayed; his saliva
unrolled like parchment. He had
the rigid arms of a firewatcher. I wanted
to know if he was Israeli or Palestinian.
I wanted to ask him the most obvious question,
"Have you ever been to Jerusalem before?"

I kept seeing the sign as we sped
down the freeway. *I lost my home . . .*
My heart moved to stone, fists
dropped quick to pale fingers,
and imagination shut like a trunk,
heavy, alone,
then it briefly opened
before we reached the Old City
and teetered near the Mount of Olives
rolling into exhaustion and dust,
lost my home . . .

Supplication

Alone, some place between
a wild raspberry patch
and a remote copse of trees,
kneeling on a cloth of pine needles
under a lean-to of my own making
with dirt in one hand and a thread of might
in the other—while a dash
of bird song scissors in my ears—
I bow beneath the air's
origin and feel my breath

course into it like a stream heading
straight for a river or a meteor
diving into the sea. It is not enough
to close my eyes in this pleading
and think of marble statues or offer
up the lyre within, as if it were full
of balancing notes and wistful symphonies.
No, no, but maybe it's enough

to scrape my knees
in this far flung closet,
to think more of Milton near the end
than Pound in church,
and to feel my left hand
sink into the earth, while my right
hand disconnects, perhaps even disappears
in the flame of the rising sun.

Burial

Summer Wish from a Bedouin Tent

I want to clamp down
on the whole of it—

this sound somewhere between shot-
gun and helicopter

zipping past my lips, chattering
into the Beersheva night.

David, Marwan, and I circle this tent,
yell a *hamdillilah* and *baruk ha-shem*

before we speak too much
of meeting in the fields like soldiers

or hitchhikers or students left
to ask questions during one more lecture.

(Someone, get us all a glass of water.)

I'd like to think it would be enough
to listen in this lantern light

with sand massaging our toes
and a new prayer being offered up

from somewhere, and maybe
the siren in an ancient voice will choke our own,

once, twice, even a third time,
and around the fifth we'll barely nod

or think of words like *bullet* or *bomb*.
I want a Mediterranean lullaby

(amidst this Holy Land fight)

in this cistern night. I want
to spread like olive oil bathing the ground

and forget the history we know
when pretending to discuss current events.

Perhaps none of us should speak.

Beneath the Falls

I slip in a pool
below water falling like shards.
A humming vortex
churns mosquitoes, sticks,
dead skin, minnows, a spot
where forces coax the moss
and ducks to dip under.
Rays of light cling
to the streaming water
before gravity snuffs them out.
Swift beads fly from the center;
the rush traces down and scatters
across the polished rocks, spraying
over roots, arrowheads, larkspur,
spinning the pupils of my eyes.
The gray dimming whirls over,
fans off my torso, spits edges
of iris, thistle, and bark
before they slough away.
Quickly, it buries me
with the bodies of lizards and stars.

Sweetness

November sun melts the end zone's ice,
pushes back the freeze.
Soldier Field salutes a quiet change
of clothes, ham strings, jersey 34
as the stands rumble with black
and blue screams. I gaze

into replays of his outstretched hand
and watch his smile tug at the light,
lingering, on a jaw that ignores
the defensive fog. He cuts away
from the sidelines, levels Matt Blair
with a block. He hands the game ball
to a fan like a runner passing the baton.

I wonder why no lineman
could hold him down
for more than two seconds—
such quarter weight, shot gun bead,
tires spurning. How easy it is
to watch the memory and not life. On TV
I see the crowd chanting: *Win one for Walter.*
I want to promise I'll play that way,
I want to promise I'll run through the hits
and go the 4th down distance.
In my front yard I pick up
a white headband and slippery leaf.
My body straddles the Midway.
My mind rises in the autumn air.

Alive Serious

Dancing on the hospital bed
after the doctors mentioned remission,
Todd thought of the Bee-Gees, the dead
one whose face was lost in bliss

after the doctors mentioned remission,
and they said the weekend was Todd's
to go to the park or get lost in the bliss
of a new film. Too much time was

in view when they said the weekend was his
to escape from the white walls,
to see a new film and feel how he was
rescued from the empty halls

of medicine, and now fleeing the walls,
up against the taxi horns and mime shtick
forgetting those empty halls,
he tried not to care where he spit.

Yet there went everyone doing their shtick
turning when loose change danced
on the ground next to the spit.
There's always a chance . . .

yet no one thought that maybe his dance
was an excuse or premature.
Still, there's a slight chance,
he thought and accepted the lure

regardless if it was premature.
Besides, the Bee-Gees weren't all dead.
He felt his body cast out like a lure
and thought of dancing on his hospital bed.

Letulogy

Uncle Howard,

At sixty, your traces stalk the hollows
of grocery stores from here to Snowflake,
Arizona. A thatch of curly gray hair
shuttles past the cash register, your cow-
milking hands pull a list out of an empty wallet.
You are forever in the next aisle over,
shaking a watermelon, picking at your
mustache, laughing with the manager
over an inside joke concerning paper or plastic,
laughing through the vegetables of loneliness
and the continual grind of bare freezers
and birthdays without anything, not even a cake.
Today it's a flannel shirt
I see slipping through sliding glass
doors. Something lost in the hunter's
worn down red, a familiar set of stripes
running through the plaid. Tomorrow
in San Diego your fingerprints will appear
on a drinking fountain, and in two weeks
a phone call will arrive from Oahu,
full of guttural questions and sun.

Yet it's always yesterday
I imagine you near the backwoods
of Oklahoma, opening large stable doors,
then brushing the mane of a palomino
as a bird warbles through the muffled dawn.
You submerge in growing
light, occasionally smiling at nothing
near the end of the street.
You pat the horse and speak
secrets into a flickering ear.

From here I have only this letter
I'm not sure where to send
or this eulogy I am too afraid to speak.
Perhaps, tonight I'll return
to an obscure shelf in the grocery store,
buy couscous or ask a stranger
to explain the difference between
writing to the disappeared
and speaking to the dead.
That's when I'll envision you
again carrying a saddle
into another hazy morning,
that's where the picture fades,
where the horse lowers its head,
eats what's left out of your hand.

Love,

Mark

Denial

What is easy to know
arrives alone and incandescent,
long after a sermon or fight.
The mind grows clear as water
beneath the mid-May sun.
And then, at night
when sorrow and guilt
dangle on cerebral pulleys
so the curtain can't descend,
release and movement
open doors and keys
are common as salt.
Despite the clarity
and crumpled friction
the face hitches to a screen.
Ears burn for Drs. Phil
and Laura, for the thrum
of Internet speed, the habits
of New Year's Eve.
Hardwired mechanics
hunch the body before long
to stoic indecision
or a slump before a slot machine.
Somehow I still trick myself
in the recess between mental
gifts and physical lethargy
to hike over what's known
to what I may regret—

the rattle of opening night,
the Chorus' painted face,
rows of bodies
with their yawns and yaps—
to the banner of what could
but does not change.

Grass

Merges with the squirrel's grin.
Rows of it in teeth. Rises from crew cut
to reveal ponytail,
then waves in the wind,

claims, *This is how we do it. This is how
we return*. Bows again as if to make stronger.
Bows again as if on stage.
A blade, a blade, a blade—
each one, child or convict, rearing up.

Spindle after spindle points the way,
or hides the unseen snake
from the sandbox child.
Crowded, yet defers to dandelion's curls.
Lifts weeds to sky. Nostril ping.

Going to dew. Available: its beard
of loam, its spinal fluid, the swelter
that wears it down. Stolid, blind,
or stammering. The soft spin
of a badminton net . . . all the routine.

Again; surging, tickle on the neck,
prayer that stains the knees. The night
crawlers underneath.
The flare of end zone comatose in winter.
Sunbathers offered to the light.

On the Anniversary of Your Death

Dear Brian,

When people ask how many
siblings I have, I stew over three
and camp near four. Either way,
I keep the nest close, shield
your three years from the outside:
especially the time when your feet,
heavy with caked mud
and the bite of May
tripped in dew as you ran
past the lifeguard and broken bottles,
beyond the gnats whining above.
You scared the ducks in green fever,
rolled in the churning of wet ground.
Church mothers carried you
from the air of an empty swing
as your jungle grin turned lean
in sandbag cheeks. How dripping
and taut the echoes, ragged the stars.

Brother, come run the park
if you misunderstand. Wring my neck
with your pudgy hands. I see
your fingers swell like worms
after a heavy rain. My heart is beating:
kiss it better.

Love,
Mark

Semblance

The last gleam of evening
dusts off the back deck
clear and smooth as the *Pietá*
while the sun lingers in its descent
like a drop of water
hanging to the end of a pine needle.
In the silence, Mary's reflection
shimmers in the windowpane—
that twisted yet knowing face,
the bowed head tied to the heart's sword,
that piercing memory of what Simeon said
in the harsh Jerusalem twilight.
I scan the deck as if somehow
there might appear the body of Jesus,
and for a moment,
all I can see is the streamlined grain
of wood, the triangular patterns
following one another like a series
of arrowheads or spear tips, interrupted
by the misshaped knot
I can't help but touch:
this inordinate projection like a bruised eye
or a back's welt, these rough edges
stained with meaty varnish,
this bleeding crown,
this scar headed for my heart.

Rabbi, Where Dwellest Thou?

JOHN 1:38

Beyond the far hill, past the ridge of sight,
approaching the silvered clip of bird song
and the repose of olive trees at night,
close to the moth-eaten, a few furlongs
from the line of common wares and chatter,
the mired janglings, the trumpeting fasts,
surging wine vats, winds of sweet savour,
by the stuttering and stolen, the grass-
hoppers and calves, frankincense and frontlets,
between the gum and thorn of acacia,
among branch and root, torment and regret,
in the command and cloak of Elisha,
facing the wilderness and Galilee.
Gird yourself as we go, come and see.

Spirit

At the worn yet polished pulpit,
in the contradiction of February's snowfall
and thaw, she adjusted her gypsy shawl,
gasped into the microphone, clutched the podium
with blotchy hands, those hands that scrubbed,
for years, what the rest of us left
under the pews, beside the trash cans,
our rings and watches next to the bathroom sinks
—and what left her lips was not warlike flare,

nor the jasper shock of bloodstone,
neither was it the pastoral turned tirade
of a patriotic afternoon. It was the quiet
lift of the Samaritan, Rahab's offer
of protection for protection, the alabaster box
for head and feet, reins and heart,
and what kept coming, not quite reeling,
was unmeasured, almost obscure, and whatever
it was it unfolded like a leaflet,

unrolled like a Persian rug. It whirred
like the touch of a cardinal's wings.
It kept offering the altar of incense,
an evening's watch, forgotten psalms;
it unhinged the door of my traditions,
wiped away the veneer on my face,
dried up those hidden wells of anger,
brought myrrh to the corridors
of sickness. My sins arose in flame.

Alteration

The Dark Room

I sit here in the dark room.
It is so silent
it makes me think
I rest at the base of a maple tree.
I turn the music on
a little ways
and lie down like a dead bird.
All the colors start to change.

Straightway

We left the shekels and docks, boats and nets,
the absent-minded sling of fish too small
and fair reprieve at the end of a day,
which says nothing of the other assets:
the ivory and couches, lamb and rock walls,
friends and their gilded attempts at wordplay,

but then letting go settled in, routine
yielded to parables and words that trawl
for heart and body, words we could not weigh
but came to us pared down, unshaped, serene—
like clay.

Silent Wednesday

Somehow in the strident ring
of markets and limestone
and the effervescent thrust of mid-morning,
the slosh of rejoinders and missed sales,
and the continuous niggling
of those who hunched over the law
like it was their final meal,

you avoided the press
of those trying to translate
miracles into Beelzebub and madness,
of those feigning melancholy
and rectitude among the masses

under the Mount Moriah sun.
You authored the final act
of scribal silence,
your own scroll
untainted, purer than gypsum,
waiting for the heft and diatribes,
taunts and spittle,
hanging
on for the slow march of prophecy,
the work of flesh and earth
alone in the will of the Father,
hidden away in Bethany,
girding yourself
for the coronation
to come.

Seeing Someone I Used to Know

She walks with others
across the chapel, her voice
trailing through the pews,
hovering like a wisp of candlelight.
I take my place at the heart's dais,
wonder about the years spread out
between us, the grass clippings,
the hailstones, the curtains just touching
the windows. Like the janitor,
I remain unnoticed,
debate whether to interrupt
the jostling of goodwill
or the smile connected
to an index finger. She continues
her reverie, her whisperings,
her petitions lifting with the rise
of shoulders and songs. The past
caroms me to the organ pipes, the sacrament
table, the bishop's gray jacket,
leads me to think of others
I've just barely met.

And it's not because of shame
or fear or even the desire
to stay unseen that prevents me
from seeing how her life
has come to pass. And it's not
because I'm unfeeling or disinterested
in my friend's good keeping.
It's a matter of control
and yielding to time,
allowing history to surprise me
without commentary and justification
as I take and eat the bread,
knowing, regardless of the week
or season of worship,
my past will arrive quietly
in an unchosen hour
warming, perhaps bowing,
like a taper flickering
at what once was
and who we used to be.

Holding it Together

I work on the driveway filling the cracks
with concrete and mortar,
the street empty, but the backyard
teeming with children's voices.

They are more beehive than bully barn,
but still, they come from different climates
and chambers. They sound part flute,
part percussion. They don't know the texture

yet of signed papers and only the oldest
knows of the boy who recently took his life.
Once I nodded to his father. Once I heard
him speak wind and miracles

to a large hall of students. Then I felt
his refrain in my own words
to a similar tribe. This afternoon
I wish I said something more

than mundane fiction and heard the inside
of his son's spliced heart before it was
too late. I can only feel the friction
of sadness troweling over new concrete,

wishing I could clear it all
or wash it away, but knowing
now I can only give it time, time
to hold the weight together and dry.

I am here, Lord.

ACTS 9:10

Tonight in the gall
of wonder, I remember
his eyes, at once two pits and torches,
scales gleaming in all that blindness,
my fingers trembling on his head.
Those pits return in the full light of day
when I'm alone with heat
and parchment dry as bone. They return
me to the gate, to the home of Judas
at *Derb el-Mustaqim*, bright as swords
or Roman shields left
beneath the afternoon sun. He returns
in dreams like he's crossing
the Galilee, the passage
of one teacher to another, the wool cloth
wound into a blanket, the camel
leaving the wilderness to drink. I want

to believe in the water's silver purge,
in the simultaneous burial and shimmer of flesh,
in the quick rending of the heart, the hearts
of those I presume to know
and try to shake from the altar of regret,

yet how I expect the taut brow of history
and hesitate when approaching what's undone,
plowed, and clean,
what's so full of foundation and witness,
that even my mind looks for traces
of what used to be. He who once
came to bind, who came like hail
out of season, now winds like sweet grass
leaning toward the sea—this lion ready
to run. His increase tugs at my praise and envy
yet.

Totality

AUGUST 21, 2017 (REXBURG, IDAHO)

It was like dying and coming back. Imagine
the sun's corona flared and silvered
around the moon's sable oval, like satin

in some apocalyptic dimension.
Kids and teens screamed, even adults skirled,
accepted what they couldn't imagine

of the sky as both angel and demon.
All thoughts left to unravel or unfurl
like hollow to hem of a dress made of satin.

Two minutes of rapture and transfiguration
turned the moon into refuge and black pearl.
Breaths lapsed like those scaling Everest, I imagine.

The west no longer owned the horizon.
In each direction, violet and amber whirled
while stars burnished brighter than satin.

The ancients must have wondered, *What happened
to the borders of this predictable world?*
All of us there died and came back. Imagine
the moon's surface enshrined in celestial satin.

Playing Ball at Church

My brother shoots the ball
as if the rim is an altar,
and the net is Belgian lace,
as if somehow, a torch will
appear and light itself
in his coach's chalky hands,
as if the leather in its spiral
and three-point arc
is a rain-making prayer
after four seasons of drought.
When my brother shoots, there is
silence, no lip curling, trash talk,
no arm swinging bravado, he shoots
as if to send you headfirst
through the net, nylon and cotton
like surplice against your cheeks,
as if after the shot a fire
fills your elbows and wrists.
My brother shoots as if holiness
can exist in any place, as if
beside his court the crowd revives
and you can hear its molten,
resurrected breath.

Ironman

Here is the nimbus
    and tempo of it all:
        Listen for whorl
as it hits the ocean's mile markers,
    find the music of mid-morning,
        salsa brimming over
Panama City,
    merengue humming
        in the shells on the beach.
Think Munich 1972.
    Not terrorists or *danke schön*.
        Think shaggy, sable hair
and streamed lines
    in the arms and mustache of Mark Spitz.
        Ease into the mantra of scripture
or Hare Krishna,
    brace yourself for the stride
        of talisman and prophet.
Keep an eye on the tow-headed ones
    behind you. They think
        they know Daltrey's refrain,
but you are the one
    who *won't get fooled again*.
        As you feel the bike's canter,

beware the mirage of skaters,
   the Lance Armstrong look-a-likes
     the ease in the Florida keys.
And if you should come upon
   remnants of gator or live oak
     or allamanda, if you should skirt
hurricane-downed power lines
   and inhale the nectar
     of bougainvillea
or recall your sons' faces
   as they neared the end
     of their 50-miler last summer
you'll feel upwelling
   tap the last strains of glucose
     in your sinews, your wrists.
Take those strands
   through the day's last light,
     beyond goo, headbands,
and ocean's pummeling surf.
   You are spear or arrow
     in the palm's ratty quiver.
You are Salazar and Bikila
   in the gum-eyed stretch,
     and when the earlobes go sallow,
when the salt on your chin
   is more than mere crust,
     when your mind turns to Mud Lake,

welcome the hallucinations
     and their burnings,
          hail mustard fever
and the throat's
     white patches of thrush,
          praise Goethe
at the 86th corner
     when he surprises you
          with some Cuban tones
in a palm tree specter,
     Do not hurry;
          do not rest.

The Language of Conversion

When coming up out of the baptismal font
you learned to breathe
in a language of water and blood,
beehives and oxen,
persecution and temple stone.

Over time, your breath turned
to words soft as a Maori whisper
and large as palm fronds
which then became the voice

of covenant and Chile, your tongue
memorizing your father's participial
phrases, your banter and knowledge
growing as certain as the longest

coastline in the world.
Your language developed into its own
family of husband, four daughters,
and one son, each more complicated
than the Altaic, simpler
than playground versions of Morse code.

Gradually, almost imperceptibly,
it evolves into the Adamic and Evic
where the soaring flames of your voice
lift, and will continue to lift,
like an oratorio out of your body.
No one will misunderstand then
the grand intention of your choices.

All of it will appear
like a pure and faithful translation,
and even the meekest will shout
like scholars did when they deciphered
the hieroglyphics on the Rosetta stone.

My Brother's Bed

To wake up remembering his empty bed
is serene as touching the walls of a cave,
is to believe you can keep that Friday in mind
and heft Galilee on your back.
To hang up the night's smock
and oil the lamp, to see through
a blinding tear is to step outside of a day
and allow whoever knocks on the front door
to visit you in this upstairs corner room
you call your childhood. This place
that returns today and on a Friday ten years hence,
occupied now by someone else's brother
who makes that room his windowed attic,
his foyer of the sky.

Praise

Pregnancy

For forty-five months out of nine years
of marriage, the squirm of joint
and muscle, elbow and kick swung

beneath your ribs, caused you to pause
some mornings at the base of stairs.
In the welling up of your belly,

such twisting legs and aching flesh,
such wispy, scarecrow knuckles
were enough to drive you into afternoons

of slumber. Not one month, or one week,
was less important than the others
as distending nerves continued to stiffen

your back and sharpen your ears
for the nights of catnaps to follow.
Always, you braced as the interior world

wound up its knock, when you offered
your body to its own deep rivers
and treacherous streams, to those slippery,

trilling words: *bear down, push,*
one more time; this journey is ineluctable.
Yet even now, years later, you understand

how those many months
pulled you outside of yourself
while the rest of us looked on, in stupor

and wonder, waiting for the fire and aura
of the flexible crown, the streaked body,
the colored cord, the life.

Arrival—Fall 2001

When you arrived in charcoal October,
we swept up every last hairball and mote,
scrubbed the pine floor into a fine shimmer
and wiped down the bulk of our winter coats.
When you arrived that wind-burned afternoon
we'd heard the jangle of Harry Potter,
Ron, Snape, and Hermione, but their tune
in our ears was faint whistle and simmer.
When you arrived we appeased the doctor's
desire for sleep, giving up our own
in the smoldering ashes of terror,
fallen towers, remains of skin and bones.
It was mercy to rock with you at night,
to touch your hair in the soft, morning light.

Back

In early morning, as you run down the hall
tumbling over the rug, clutching a stuffed animal,
I can't help but toss you over my shoulder,
your fly-away curls blind
both of us, your squeals sling down
my ear, the notes peal
sharper than winter air.

You hop down and toe into the kitchen,
pleased that I now understand your raised finger,
your whispered plea, *Cup of milk, cup of milk.*

You came into our lives like a bird
flying out of a magician's fiery pot.
Your wings and rhythms forming somewhere else.
What did you do with what you left behind?
Are scarves and jump ropes winding you
through an ante-mortal wormhole or tipping point?

For you, the only tip is a head moving forward,
no going back to a fist in the mouth
or smacking gums or cells quick
to divide.

Yet occasionally I go back,
attempting to piece together
your essence with the verbal splashes
I hear now.
How a blueprint exists for each house
and a mathematician knows the endlessness of a line.
Even when you aren't here,
I still hear footsteps
down the hall.

First Day of School

On the cusp of reading, spelling,
you parse out delicate rhythms
to the pulse of memory,
submerge in the granite of language,

attune to scale, tone, even nuance
amidst the nascent seedbed of thought.
In you resounds the rhapsody of the garden:
the exalted twists of root and leaf,

the undercurrent of corm and node.
Your hair suggests both mixing soil
and flourishing vine: a benison in winter,
a weight under the roiling sun; your voice

lines with the hills of negotiation, the ones
you ride through the eye of the storm.
On this beginning, I would give,
if I could, a pause for each emotion,

a gesture for every stirring, a comet
to carry you over the evening dark.
Yet the best I can do abounds
in the invisible strand of blessing:

that you'll continue to learn
more from the bow than the arrow,
know the spontaneity of pepper,
preserve the healing in salt,

believe that far flung need
casts pall over mountainous want.
Yes, olive one, 'this acceptance take'
as you embrace the literate world

in all its roadmaps, forms, flurries.
Hoe in this garden for thresholds
or vast secrets; then, you'll better understand
what to gather, what to leave in the sun.

The Reader

This afternoon, my seven-year-old, rests
on the couch, balancing
Harry Potter and The Half-Blood Prince
between her knees. She reads the way
fish can swim, the way monkeys
sling from branch to branch.
Each spare moment the book,
almost any book,
props up her Mexican forehead
and swift imagination.

And always, she moves from text
to reason to queries,
revealing precise meanings
like an atlas or the *Oxford English Dictionary*.
Most days the ritual continues:
The printed word, soft cushions, exact questions.
Each year authors envision her—
the one not afraid to swim away
in the murky and mysterious depths,
the one looking in on the rest of us
from her position
in the wild vines of the trees.

Fifth Set

After nine months of estrogen, after
they rush to the hospital, mid-morning,
to witness unfolding, the nurse banter
with the doctor, clinical auguring,
she closes her eyes, foregoes the spinal
block to forge kinship with hosts of women
and her rising son, her fifth child, the final
note, akin to a blunt, tingling *Amen*,
or like the pound and heave in the fifth set:
the whale arc and splash for the dipping ball,
the crosscourt volley, then overhead stream,
bruise in the tailbone, nothing left to sweat
just one more dive amid the muscles' gall
when she hears him open his mouth and scream.

Sacrament

End of January: my future wife
shakes my hand in between
church services. She holds it,
asking for my last name
as if in the answer lies
a brainteaser or crossword puzzle.

I think of saying *Rothstein* or *Greene*,
Mecklenberg or *Gambel*, but all
I can muster is stuttering truth,
a veracious slip of the tongue
that reflects more ego
than id, not some drafty
pick-up line like, "Kiss me if I'm wrong,
but don't I know you?"

Several Januaries later,
it's hard to know whose holding
whose hand in church. We stare
and nod at each other,
absorb the silence of communion,
adjust the children on both sides of us
as trust fixes one palm to the other
like our names spoken together,
like body and bread, vine and leaves.

To a Daughter Warning a Friend

At mid-freshman year, any ninth grader
can hear gossip, whispered or otherwise,
a mile away from shop class
and peers' real or perceived issues, eventually,
resound across the Upper Snake River Valley
like a mad wind on a March afternoon.
Most of the blather settles in the lunchroom
or gymnasium air. Even so,
amid all the tie-dyed slobber and candy clamor,
you discerned her shaky hand
as it sent texts, you didn't ignore
the breach in her voice,
her vibrato warbling
through a faux bravado, an online
Canadian trap ready to spring for her
like a bear emerging from hibernation.

Because of you, she didn't dis home
or gamble on a stranger's tip.
Maybe you've shrugged off
that you saved her
from some unknown lackey,
some horseradish heavy breather
whose viscous fingerprints stay concealed
behind a two-bit computer screen.
Maybe you worried you'd end up

the only nark in school. But you must know,
tonight she rests in a swirl of song
and clear air, propping her feet up,
looking out the back door
to a sun setting in peace and probability.
What is a friend, but a sign
posting notice of uneven ground
or a hidden canal? You gave her
the cloak of amity and token
of bravery, gifts allowing her and you
to know the contours of conscience
and the rest that comes
from days, even years, of deep, deep sleep.

Recap

Moments of dribbling rebound
into your mind now that the season
is over. Such replays steal in

like the night you first shut down
the opposing team's best player.
Memory soothes and comforts, conjures

an O on the inside of your lips.
Yet, memory, too, can coax
you out of thinking a pass was better

than it actually was, can push you out
of getting too secure with a seat
on the bench. Memory isn't merely

high-fives and waving towels. If you
listen, it's telling you you're tougher
than the bolts and glass holding up

the rim. It's the maturing, future story
that shows you'll find, eventually,
the open lane and assures you'll take

another foul shot. Memory means you're
not just a believer anymore. You're
an answered prayer, sealing your opponent

against trouble and her own flat feet, waving
for the overhead pass, reaching with open
arms and hands for whatever comes next.

Good Friday

You polish the silverware and bowls,
arrange appliances and cords
along the kitchen counter until the line
between cleanliness and purity,

so pressed and scrubbed,
is as fragrant as the opening
of an Easter lily. Who would
figure that late March

in its rumblings—awash in canyon wind
and matted, yellow grass—could be
so aromatic. When I come home
there seems to be an oratorio

in the background, rising clarinets
preparing for a flare of trumpets.
Today the water is turning to wine,
and the silver coin gleams in the distance

as we place a few lilies
among the necessities, a sparkle
between cables and hardware, a skosh
of sun and air, gold and translucent.

Braiding My Daughter's Hair

Yes, it's no secret, I've categorized
      in the name of art,
husbandry, and even survival. I've divvied up

dish washing and lawn mowing
      trash hauling
and lamb simmering into the fortresses

labeled *Men* and *Women*, but weeks ago
      in the helter-skelter
of words and ablutions prior to family

photos, I stretched past the worn
      corners of stereotypes
and gathered three, thick strands

of my teenage daughter's hair, one lock
      streaming like the River Wye,
the other almost singing, purling like the Rio

Bravo. Now, I have crossed the Columbia
      and floated down sections
of the Snake, I've sent my mind headlong

over the Mississippi and made it to the edge
        of Jordan, but the middle tress
of her mane was the river her mom and I

once dreamed about, a conduit of autonomy,
        an unofficial *quinceanera*,
the gentle center of Welsh, Mexican,

and independent genes, channeling into the ocean
        of birthright and adulthood—
this strand propelling me beyond label

and convention, beyond the Dutch or French
        braid into her own sovereignty
of where's she's been and what she hopes to be.

Holding Your Hand in Bed

Not so much a grasp or parking spot
but ease and extension—
an under-the-sheets covert
from devices and steering wheels
after the smoky years
of shuttling kids and re-figuring spreadsheets
and weeding in the garden
of pasts and possibilities.
Both of us like baseball gloves
softening in the other's hand.

Considering What's Undone

I'll hear incessant ringing
of the phone after dinner
or watch the simultaneous nod
and "Uh-huh" when I ask, "Who's texting?"

and of course the initial interrogation
masked by handshake and smile
just before the homecoming dance.
I'll fight haze before sleep

as I hear you tiptoe past curfew and through
the front door, but then the cost
of a first job interview and calculus,
let alone insurance, and the invective

in your journal about breaking out
of this popsicle town and pulling one over
on your navvy parents who've forgotten
how to skip rocks across water.

I'll look away from prosaic news
when you tug at the corners
of the living room couch
and can't bring yourself to say, "Dad,"

how it hurts to swallow before you speak.
All you manage are tears
at the lost playoff game
and shaky hands ripping

the form letter of the unoffered scholarship,
yet I'll hear you wake at 4:00 a.m.
to hike mountains and train
for triathlons, your aura lighting

up the kitchen in the deep freeze
of January. You'll rope a sibling
from the cliff's edge and provide
a safe landing to the man

with a broken parachute. From our backyard
to Canada, across Italy and around the Cape
of Good Hope, you'll feel earth
and firmament push you

into the headwinds of someone new,
someone I'll keep reaching toward
as my knees give way to worn tendons
and torn ligaments, even as I hold

your children on Thanksgiving
or Easter or a random afternoon.
In their faces, I'll see swimming pool
creases and umber birthmarks,

smattering of ancestral patterns
in their hairlines and reach, their
voices echoing the canned and idiosyncratic,
and I won't have to listen for it,

I'll simply hear it in piano recitals
and extra-inning baseball games, the thrum
of innocence and resiliency. I'll hear you
forge into their bodies the swift current

of habit and discipline as they flow down
the street into vast prisms of rain
and sunshine, remnants of you always
emerging, vestiges I love and know.

www.ingramcontent.com/pod-product-compliance
Lightning Source LLC
LaVergne TN
LVHW051701080426
835511LV00017B/2672